PORSCHE

PORSCHE

Andrew Noakes

p

This is a Parragon Publishing Book

First published in 2005

Parragon Publishing
Queen Street House
4 Queen Street
Bath BA1 1HE, UK

A copy of the CIP data for this book is available from the British Library upon request.

The rights of Andrew Noakes to be identified as the author of this work have been asserted in accordance with Section 77 of the Copyright, Designs and Patents Act of 1988.

Created, designed, produced and packaged by Stonecastle Graphics Ltd

Designed by Paul Turner and Sue Pressley
Edited by Philip de Ste. Croix

Photographs © LAT Photographic Digital Archive

Printed and bound in Malaysia

The author and publishers have made every reasonable effort to contact all copyright holders. Any errors that may have occurred are inadvertent and anyone who for any reason has not been contacted is invited to write to the publishers so that a full acknowledgement may be made in subsequent editions of this work.

ISBN: 1-40545-252-8

Page 1: Three generations of Porsche. Clockwise from front: 1980s 924 Carrera GT, 1960s 356C, 1970s 911 Carrera RS.

Page 2: The classic 911 shape was gently modernized for the 964 and this, the 993 series.

Page 3: Porsche dominated sports car racing in the 1980s with the 956 and 962 cars.

CONTENTS

INTRODUCTION 6

CHAPTER 1
BUILDING THE LEGEND 8

CHAPTER 2
THE CLASSIC 911 24

CHAPTER 3
CHANGING DIRECTION 42

CHAPTER 4
MODERN DAYS 56

CHAPTER 5
LEADING THE PACK 76

INDEX 96

The 375bhp GT3 RS was the last of the

996-series 911s.

INTRODUCTION

Porsche is one of the most evocative names in motoring, and with good reason. Professor Ferdinand Porsche designed innovative and effective cars for some of the great racing marques, including Daimler, Auto Union, and Cisitalia, not to mention the most popular people's car of them all, the legendary Volkswagen. And then, in 1948, Porsche started producing sports cars under his own name.

This first Porsche road car, the 356, was based on modified Volkswagen components. Despite those humble origins it quickly won a giant-killing reputation, and ever larger flat-four engines made the cars quicker and quicker. By 1953 Porsche was racing special quad-cam 550 Spyders, which were almost unbeatable in their class. Later in the 1950s Porsche progressed into Formula 2 single-seater racing, and briefly tried Formula 1 (winning one Grand Prix) before concentrating on sports cars and sports car racing – and a brand new road car.

Porsche's seminal 911 was launched in 1964 and the same basic car, though much refined, was still on sale a quarter of a century later. Originally fitted with a 2.0-liter flat-six engine, the 911 would receive bigger and bigger engines, tuned and turbocharged, and develop into a sports car icon. The 911's performance and efficiency, its classic good looks, and its impeccable build quality, represented everything Porsche stood for – and even for Porsche's own engineers, it proved to be a tough act to follow.

But the Porsche story is about more than just the 911. It's also about increasingly sophisticated sports racing cars – the all-conquering 917 in Europe and the incredibly powerful 917/30 in Can-Am racing. It's about the 936, 956, and 964 sports racers which won so often at Le Mans, and the TAG-Porsche engines which dominated Formula 1. And the Porsche road-car story encompasses successive new generations of cars to carry the 911 badge, together with sports cars from the relatively affordable to the outrageously expensive – each one adding to the legend that is Porsche.

By 1958 Porsche had incorporated numerous revisions into a model called the 356A, and a 1.6-liter four-cam engine was available in this, the Carrera 1600GS. Earlier Porsche four-cam engines with roller-bearing crankshafts had been temperamental, if powerful, but this new 1586cc unit reverted to plain bearings and a new design of conrod, and it gave a reliable 105bhp.

CHAPTER ONE

BUILDING THE LEGEND

Ferdinand Porsche was 73 when his company started making its own sports cars. After an early interest in electrical power, Porsche had worked for Austro-Daimler, then for the Daimler company in Germany, before setting up in business as an independent design consultant. The 1934 Auto Union P-wagen racing car, which set the pattern for modern single-seaters, was one early project. Another was the design of a 'people's car,' which after the war became the Volkswagen.

Porsche's own sports cars derived from the Porsche Type 64, a design for a small racing coupé based on Volkswagen mechanical parts – which meant a steel platform chassis, leading- and trailing-arm suspension, and a rear-mounted, flat-four engine with air cooling. War intervened and the Type 64 never raced, but the fundamental idea of building a sports car using Volkswagen components would resurface in 1947, as the Type 356 – designed by Porsche's son, Ferry.

Early 356s were built at the Porsche Design workshops in Gmünd, Austria, but by 1950 production had moved to the Zuffenhausen district of Stuttgart. Standard coupé bodies were built by the nearby Reutter concern, but several other coachbuilders also contributed their own coupé and roadster versions. The horizontally-opposed, four-cylinder engine of the Volkswagen was tuned and expanded, from 1086cc to 1286cc and then to 1488cc, using a special built-up crankshaft. By then Porsche 356s were making their name around Europe and in the US.

Fast and lightweight, the cars proved popular in competition, and a purpose-built racing sports car, the 550 Spyder, followed in 1953 – and proved highly competitive in its class. It was one of these cars which American film star James Dean was driving when he died in a road accident in 1955.

As successive versions of the 356 became faster, more reliable, and more refined, so the Porsche name became renowned as one of top builders of sports cars. The legend had begun.

RACING START

Porsche designed the Volkswagen Type 64 (above) for
the Berlin-Rome-Berlin road race in 1939, but the
coming of war meant the race never took place. But
the plan for a sports car based on the Porsche-
designed Volkswagen engine and suspension, and the
light, aerodynamically efficient body designed by Erwin
Komenda, would not go to waste. Porsche's own
sports cars would use just this recipe after the war.

RAISING THE ROOF

Though the first prototype had been a roadster,
Porsche decided that the 'standard' 356 body would
be a fixed-head coupé. In 1950 production of 356s
began in Zuffenhausen, a district of Stuttgart. The
bodies, built by the nearby Reutter company, were
slightly reshaped to improve their appearance and
were now pressed in steel rather than hand-beaten
from aluminum alloy (right).

AUSTRIAN ENTERPRISE

The first car built under Porsche's own name was the 356, and this is the first 356 (above) – built at Porsche Design's workshops in Gmünd, Austria late in 1947. Very different from the production cars which followed, this car had a tubular steel chassis and an 1131cc Volkswagen flat-four engine placed ahead of the rear wheels. But it was the first step on the road to the production 356.

COMING TO AMERICA

Heinrich Sauter built a lightweight 356 roadster in 1951, and an alloy-bodied 'production' version was readied for 1952 at the insistence of US importer Max Hoffman. But Glaser, the coachbuilder which produced the bodies, was suffering financial problems and less than 20 of these attractive 'America Roadsters' (below) were built. It was one of the first 356s with a new 1488cc 70bhp engine, which used a special built-up roller-bearing crankshaft.

SPYDER THAT FLIES

With a light ladder-frame chassis and tuned 1500 engine, the 550 Spyder proved to be a successful sports-racing car. At Le Mans in 1953 Richard von Frankenburg and Paul Frère (number 45) won their class and finished 15th overall (above). Hard tops had been fitted in an effort to improve the 550's aerodynamics and on the long Mulsanne straight they achieved 124mph (200km/h) – but these tops also succeeded in roasting and deafening the drivers.

LIGHT FANTASTIC

The Speedster of 1954 (following pages) was an instant hit in its intended market, the USA. Built around a lightweight bodyshell, the Speedster had simplified trim and an unlined roof, together with a shorter windshield and removable sidescreens in place of the standard 356's wind-up windows. As a result the Speedster was lighter than the standard car, so performance improved, and it was also cheaper to buy – a combination which ensured its popularity.

GIANT KILLER

Porsche replaced the 550 Spyder with the Type 718 in 1957. The 718 had a new chassis design with tubes arranged in the shape of a 'K,' and as a result it became known as the RSK. After a year of development through 1957, the 718 was entered in the 1958 Targa Florio (below) where Jean Behra and Giorgio Scarlatti split the dominant 3.0-liter Ferraris, finishing second overall and winning their class. Later RS60 and RS61 versions would regularly embarrass more powerful cars.

PUSHROD POWER

The 356B of 1960 (right) included another round of detail improvements which made the cars still more appealing. The body was now taller and wider than before, and new features included the use of Alfin brake drums (which had aluminum fins bonded to the steel drum), a shorter gearlever, and a new type of synchromesh. At first there was no four-cam Carrera version of the revised car so this, the pushrod-engined Super 90, was the fastest 356B available.

The final round of improvements to the 356 came in 1963, by which time work on the 911 was well advanced. The 75bhp 356C and 95bhp 356SC (below) now had disc brakes all round, revised suspension, and better synchromesh, and these improved cars were easy to spot thanks to bigger rear windows and twin air vents in their engine covers. Road testers marveled at the SC's ability to cruise at 80–90mph (129–145km/h) with power to spare.

ABARTH ALLIANCE

A lightweight 356 two-seater was conceived for racing in 1960. Porsche supplied the 356 chassis with 1.6-liter four-cam engines, Zagato in Turin built the aluminum bodies to a design by Franco Scaglione, and final assembly was handled by Abarth. The result (above) was variously known as the Abarth Carrera or Carrera GTL (Gran Turismo Leicht, or 'light GT'). Build quality, however, was patchy, and the cars proved to be only a little lighter than a stripped-out 356 coupé.

WINNING WAYS

Jo Bonnier and Carlo Maria Abate won the 1963 Targa Florio in this 718 GTR (right), a development of the RS61 which was fitted with a flat-eight engine based on that from the now-defunct Porsche F1 car. The Porsche won by less than 12 seconds from the Ferrari of Scarfiotti, Bandini, and Mairesse, with a second Porsche driven by Herbert Linge and Edgar Barth in third place.

F2 FLING

Porsche dabbled in Formula 2 racing (above) using a central-seat version of the 718RSK sports car in 1958, winning the F2 race at Rheims that year. A proper single-seater, the 718F2, arrived the following season. After an inauspicious debut at Monaco, where Wolfgang von Trips put the car into the wall on the second lap, the F2 Porsches became race winners – and with the coming of the 1500cc Formula 1, they took Porsche into the top-level of motorsport.

ALL-AMERICAN ACE

Dan Gurney speeds over the line to win the 1962 French Grand Prix at Rouen, his and Porsche's first Formula 1 win (above). The American had driven for Porsche since 1960 and finished the 1961 F1 season in joint third place. The following year Porsche introduced the flat-eight engined 804, and Dan followed up his Rouen victory with another in the non-championship F1 race at the Solitude racetrack in Stuttgart. But Porsche's F1 campaign ended that year, the company concentrating on sports car racing instead.

The original 911 had a 2.0-liter, air-cooled, flat-six engine with 130bhp. In this, the 911S of 1967 (above), output was boosted to 160bhp using different camshafts and a higher compression ratio. Even faster 911s followed a couple of years later, when a 2.2-liter version of the flat six was introduced – giving the basic car 125bhp and the 'S' model 180bhp.

CHAPTER TWO

THE CLASSIC 911

Announced in 1963, the 911 was designed to be less cramped and more refined than its predecessors – but even quicker. Thanks to its wonderfully well-proportioned shape (penned by Ferry's son, Ferdinand Alexander) and the unceasing development it received over the subsequent years, the 911 would become a world-famous sports car icon which Stuttgart would find very difficult to surpass.

It retained the 356's rear-engined layout, but now that engine was a 2.0-liter, 130bhp flat-six. The suspension was also new – struts at front, semi-trailing arms at the rear, with torsion bars at both ends. The early cars were tricky to handle: revised weight distribution and a lengthened wheelbase helped, but the 911 would retain its reputation for scaring drivers.

At first all the cars were fixed-head coupés, but these were joined by an open-top 911 Targa in 1965, featuring a substantial fixed roll-over hoop and a removable roof panel.

The 911S of 1967 generated 160bhp from its 2.0 liters thanks to bigger valves and higher compression. The flat-six's capacity was increased to 2.2 liters in 1970 and 2.4 liters from 1972, giving the most powerful fuel-injected S versions 190bhp. In 1973 Porsche introduced the Carrera RS, with a big-bore 2687cc engine (210bhp) and a lightweight body. But even quicker 911s were just around the corner.

Porsche had already built fearsome 1000bhp turbocharged racing engines, and in 1975 a production 911 Turbo hit the streets. As if this 3.0-liter, 260bhp projectile was not enough to satisfy the most demanding of speedsters, it was followed by an even quicker 3.3-liter version in 1978.

By now the 'regular' 911 was the 3.0-liter, 180bhp 911SC, available in coupé and Targa form. A full convertible joined the range in 1982 and a 231bhp 3.2-liter Carrera arrived in 1984. By then the world had already seen the ultimate 911 in the shape of the formidable 959 – a twin-turbocharged, 450bhp supercar capable of 195mph (314km/h).

SHOW STOPPER

Porsche's successor to the 356 was announced at the Frankfurt show in September 1963 (above). Originally it was known as the 901 (as you can see from the registration plate) but Peugeot objected to the use of a three-figure number with a zero in the middle, as this had long been the French company's practice. If Porsche wanted to sell the new car in France, it had to have a different name – so it became the 911, and an icon was born.

TRACTION IN ACTION

With its engine over the rear wheels, the 911 had unbeatable traction for a two-wheel-drive car and it was a successful rally machine. Here Vic Elford and David Stone race through the night on their way to overall victory in the 1968 Monte Carlo Rally (right), ahead of the sister 911 of Pauli Toivonen and Martti Tiukkanen. Elford is the only man who has ever won the Monte Carlo Rally and finished the Monaco Grand Prix.

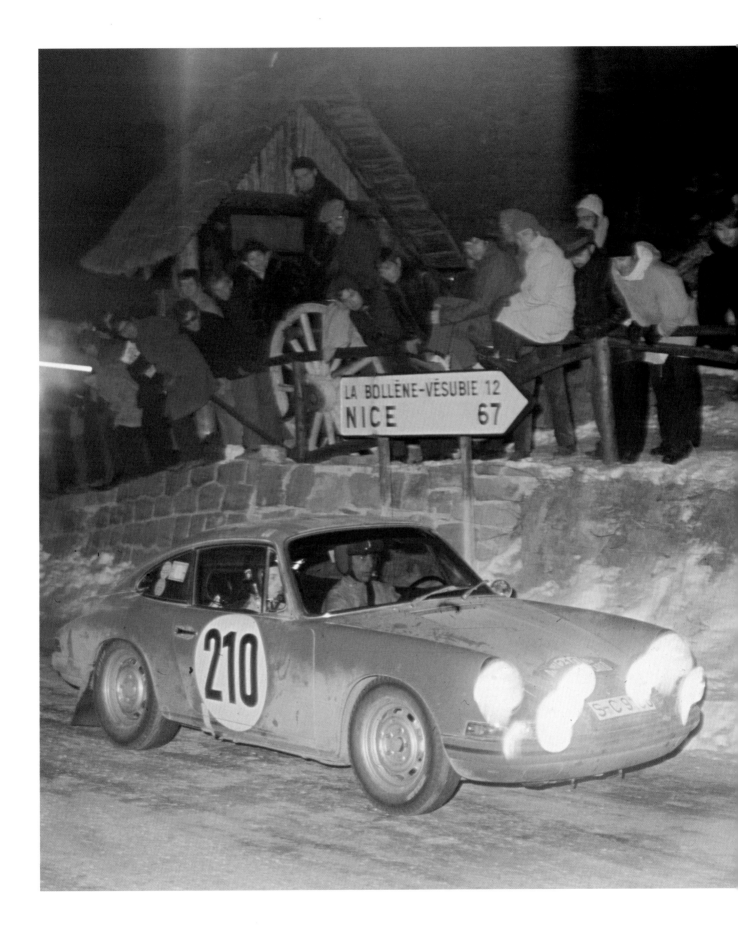

RACING CERTAINTY

*Because the 911 was produced in relatively large
numbers, and because it was a two-plus-two rather
than a two-seater, it was admitted to 'touring car'
motor racing classes which had previously been the
preserve of sports sedans and sedan-based coupés
(below). The 911 was successful in its class running
in very standard form, though it was often up against
more specialized cars like the lightweight Alfa
Romeo GTAs.*

FOUR MORE

*With the demise of the 356 in 1965, Porsche
needed a cheaper, entry-level model. By installing the
356's flat-four engine in the 911 shell it produced the
912 (right), which also had simpler trim and
equipment to keep costs down. It was a big success,
and some drivers even preferred the 912 to the 911,
claiming that the lighter engine resulted in more
forgiving handling.*

EXPANSION PLANS

The 911 engine had been deliberately designed to allow easy increases in engine capacity. From its starting point at 2.0 liters it grew to 2.2 in 1970 using a bigger bore, and then to 2.4 liters in 1972 with a longer-stroke crankshaft. In this latest form it developed up to 190bhp, and this fuel-injected 911E (below) was good for 165bhp – despite concerns over exhaust emissions regulations resulting in a reduction in compression ratio.

SPORTS SCIENCE

From a racing point of view the 911 was limited by its weight, engine size, and aerodynamic performance, all of which were addressed in the Carrera RS of 1973 (right). Lighter-gauge panels, thinner glass, and simplified interior trim saved around 220lb (100kg). The engine was bored out to 2.7 liters, generating 210bhp in production form and allowing competition versions to run full 3.0-liter engines. Finally the engine cover gained a 'duck tail' spoiler which reduced rear-end lift by 75 percent.

'R' RATED

The racing version of the Carrera RS was the RSR (left). With an even bigger (92mm) bore the RSR engine was of 2808cc capacity and used bigger ports and valves – with a 300bhp output as a result. Normally the RSR ran in racing Group 4, but modified cars with different rear suspension geometry and oversize rear spoilers ran as prototypes in the last real Targa Florio, in 1973, finishing first and third.

MAKING A MARQUE

The 911 was built at Porsche's Stuttgart-Zuffenhausen factory (above), which had previously been the home of the 356. Galvanized steel was used for some body parts from 1971, and for the entire body from 1976 – a move which required considerable investment in new welding processes. Porsche was the first car maker in the world to adopt such elaborate anti-rust measures.

GIVEN A BOOST

Porsche used turbochargers with success in its fearsome 1000bhp racing cars for the Can-Am series. In 1974 it applied the same technology to a racing 911 Carrera, and in 1975 a 911 Turbo road car hit the market with around 260bhp. In 1978 the engine was bored out to 3299cc and an intercooler added to reduce the intake charge temperatures, improving efficiency and power. The 300bhp 3.3-liter Turbo (above) was one of the fastest road cars of the 1970s.

SOLDIERING ON

*Development of the 911 slowed in the 1970s.
Porsche chief Ernst Fuhrmann believed the 911's days
were numbered and instead concentrated on the
water-cooled 924, 928, and 944 models. In 1978
the 911 range was rationalized to the Turbo and this,
the new 911SC (below), which continued until 1983.
By now the famous Fuchs forged-alloy wheels had
been replaced as standard wear by five-spoke cast
alloy wheels which were fractionally heavier – but the
Fuchs wheels were still an option.*

NEW SLANT

*The racing 935 models popularized a 'slant nose' look
for the 911 (right) – some were built to special order
by Porsche, while other versions were produced by
independent specialists. Some had 928-style fold-
forward headlamps, others used more conventional
pop-up headlamps. Without the 911's prominent fixed
lamps drag, was slightly reduced, adding a few miles
per hour to the car's top speed.*

Porsche introduced what it called a 'Targa' top in 1965. It featured a fixed roll-over hoop with a removable roof panel and a drop-down rear window (later the rear window became fixed). When the draconian safety rules that prompted the Targa design failed to materialize, a full cabriolet was planned – but it had to wait until the anti-911 Ernst Fuhrmann had retired, and 911 development had been restarted in earnest. Production began in 1982.

CLUB CLASS

In its final form the 3.0-liter 911SC had developed 204bhp, but for 1987 a more powerful engine was introduced. A more sophisticated engine management system and a rise in capacity to 3164cc (using the long-stroke crankshaft from the 3.3 Turbo) combined to produce 231bhp and still allow excellent fuel economy. Like the 2.7 RS of yore, this Carrera Club Sport (left) was treated to a weight-loss program which included deletion of the rear seats and lightweight bucket seats for driver and passenger.

THE ULTIMATE 911

Porsche unveiled its 'Group B Study' at the 1983 Frankfurt Motor Show. It was based on the 911, but the body shape was much modified with broad wheel-arch extensions front and rear to cover much wider wheels and tires. Under the skin the car incorporate a sophisticated four-wheel-drive system, and was powered by a twin-turbocharged 2.85-liter flat-six engine with liquid-cooled cylinder heads. The 200 production versions were known as the Porsche 959 (below).

The non-turbo 944 was given a boost in 1986 with a new, more powerful engine (above). Porsche designed a new cylinder head with four valves per cylinder, improving the engine's breathing ability and generating more power – up from 163bhp to 188bhp. Though they had 'only' four cylinders, all the 944 engines were very smooth because they incorporated contra-rotating balancer shafts.

CHAPTER THREE

CHANGING DIRECTION

Successful though the 911 was, it was always an expensive sports car and even the cheaper 912, with the old 356 four-cylinder engine, was out of the reach of many enthusiasts. The opportunity to put that right came at the end of the 1960s, with the introduction of the VW-Porsche 914.

Porsche designed the 914 in two versions, a 914/4 with a fuel-injected Volkswagen engine and a 914/6 with a 2.0-liter 911 unit. It had been hoped that volume sales of the VW-engined car would keep prices low, but sales were always slow. The 914/6 died out in 1972, while the 914/4 soldiered on until 1976.

It was effectively replaced by the 924, a design based on Volkswagen components which had been commissioned by VW but then abandoned by them. Never a company to let a good design go to waste, Porsche decided to put the car into production itself at the old NSU factory at Neckarsulm. Diehards complained about the use of a pedestrian water-cooled VW-Audi engine, but the 924 filled a gap in the market and proved a success – and it led to the Porsche-engined 944. Much later, the 944 was further developed into the hugely competent 968 series.

Meanwhile, as emissions regulations tightened and noise limits were continually lowered, the end seemed to be in sight for the air-cooled 911. Zuffenhausen sought to replace it with the 928, a modern Grand Touring car with a water-cooled, 4.5-liter V8 engine. Despite the 928's obvious merits, Porsche customers knew what they wanted, and what they wanted was generally the 911, so instead of replacing the old stager, the 928 ran alongside it.

Over the years Porsche gave the 928 more power, increasing the engine size to 4.6 liters, 4.9 liters, and finally to 5.4 liters in the 1991 GTS. But it never replaced the evergreen 911.

SPORTING CHANCE

Porsche collaborated with VW on the mid-engined 914 (above). It was available from 1969 in two versions, an 80bhp car powered by a Volkswagen 411E engine and a 110bhp car with the 911T engine. Though the 914 was swift and good to drive, it was never cheap enough compared to the 911, and it did not sell well. Porsche ended production of its version in 1972, though the Volkswagen-powered cars continued until 1976.

COURTING CONTROVERSY

Even after the relatively unsuccessful 914, Volkswagen wanted a sports car in its range. Porsche came up with another design using as many existing Volkswagen group components as possible, and when Volkswagen changed its mind, Zuffenhausen took over the project. It became the Porsche 924 (right), which alarmed Porsche traditionalists even more than the 914 had, because of its front-mounted, water-cooled engine – the first Porsche to use this conventional layout.

SIX APPEAL

The stillborn 916 (above) was a much more exciting car based on the 914. Where the 914 had a removable roof panel, the 916 had a fixed steel roof – but the real difference was under the engine cover, where the 916 had the top-spec 911 production engine of the time, a 2.4-liter 911S unit developing 190bhp. With less weight than a 911, the result was electrifying performance. Sadly it never reached production.

CHANGING OF THE GUARD

Porsche boss Ernst Fuhrmann was convinced that the 911 was outdated and irrelevant in an age of increasing concerns over vehicle safety and exhaust emissions, and he prompted development of a new family of water-cooled cars. One was the 924 and this, the 928 of 1977 (above), was the other. Powered by a 4.5-liter V8 it had supercar performance and exceptional refinement for a sporting car. Early interiors boasted dazzling 'op art' fabrics (right).

POWER GAMES

In typical Porsche fashion, the 924 was soon subjected to a program of development aimed at improving its performance. The first result was the 924 Turbo of 1979 (above), with a KKK turbocharger added to the Volkswagen-sourced engine, boosting power from 125 to 170bhp. The transmission and running gear were also uprated to suit. The result was a Porsche with all the performance of a 928, but at around two-thirds of the price and with considerably better fuel efficiency.

S EXPRESS

*Revisions to the 928 in 1979 produced this, the
928S (below). The engine was now 4664cc, boosting
power from the 240bhp of the early 928s to 300bhp.
External changes were limited to new wheels, an air
dam under the front bumper, and a small spoiler
under the rear window, plus rubbing strips along the
sides. Automatic transmission (supplied by Daimler-
Benz) was now standard, though a five-speed manual
gearbox was still an option.*

ALL PORSCHE

*The 924 had always been criticised for its 'non-
Porsche' engine. The answer came in 1981 when
Porsche unveiled the 944 (right), using the 924 shell
but fitted with a new, 2.5-liter four-cylinder engine –
effectively one bank of the 928's V8. With 163bhp
available the 944's all-out performance almost
matched the 924 Turbo, but because of the greater
torque of the engine at low speeds, it felt more
responsive to drive.*

THE PERFECT PORSCHE?

For 1985 Porsche applied its turbocharging know-how to the 2.5-liter in-line four in the 944. The 944 Turbo developed 220bhp, which meant that its straight-line performance was well into 911 territory. It was also a much easier car to drive fast than the rather tricky rear-engined machines. Some commentators claimed this was the

BACK TO THE FUTURE

By 1983 the 911 lobby were back in charge at
Porsche and development of the old car was once
more in full swing. But Zuffenhausen still found time to
make improvements to its line of water-cooled cars.
Numerous detail improvements went into the 928S2
(left), and Porsche began to position the V8 car as a
'Grand Touring' machine rather than as a replacement
for the 911 – as it had originally been intended.

V8 VARIETY

In 1986 the 928 was given a restyle and even more
power. The V8 engine's capacity was increased again,
this time to 4.9 liters, and new cylinder heads were
fitted with four valves per cylinder and twin overhead
camshafts on each cylinder bank. This 928GT (above),
capable of 170mph (274km/h) was the result.
In 1991 the engine was enlarged again, to 5.4 liters,
for the final 928s. The model remained in production
until 1995.

NEW KID ON THE BLOCK

The 968 (left) took over from the 944 in 1991. The new car used essentially the same body shape as the 924/944, but with a striking new nose featuring fold-forward headlamps like those on the 928. There was a choice of 3.0-liter, four-cylinder engines, a normally-aspirated unit with 240bhp and a 305bhp turbo, both with 16 valves and Porsche's VarioCam variable valve timing system.

FINAL FLING

Porsche reduced the weight of the 968 and boosted its appeal for enthusiastic drivers with the 968 Club Sport (above), introduced in the spring of 1993. The weight reduction, around 110lb (50kg), was achieved by deleting some of the non-essential equipment from the 968's specification and by fitting glassfiber-shelled racing-style seats in place of the standard items. Production of the Club Sport, and the other 968s, ended in 1995.

A new 911 GT2 appeared in 2001, following a similar formula to the previous GT2 model. That meant even more power from the turbo engine (now 465bhp) and less weight, largely by opting for rear-wheel drive instead of the Turbo's four-wheel-drive system. Bigger air intakes and bigger aerodynamic aids were also included – with a huge rear wing which the driver could adjust for the best balance of downforce and drag.

CHAPTER FOUR

MODERN DAYS

Known internally as the 964, the new 911 Carrera 4 of 1989 kept the original car's familiar shape but sought to iron out some of the problems inherent in the old design.

The engine was still an air-cooled flat-six, but now displacing 3600cc and fitted with twin ignition and variable geometry induction. It developed 250bhp, an improvement over its 3.2-liter predecessor, but more importantly it met worldwide noise and emissions regulations which were beyond the old 911.

Also new was coil spring front suspension, allowing the introduction of compliant bushes to improve ride and refinement, and four-wheel drive developed from the system that Porsche had used on 911s built for the Paris-Dakar rally. A two-wheel-drive Carrera 2, with the 964 chassis and engine but without four-wheel drive, followed a year later. A 964-shape Turbo with the old 3.3-liter engine arrived in 1991, but the definitive 360bhp 3.6-liter version came in 1993, alongside a normally-aspirated '3.8-liter' Carrera RS with 300bhp.

By 1994 the 964 had been supplanted by the 993, which still carried the 911 badge of its famous forebears. Even the lowest-powered versions could now deploy at least 270bhp, rising to 285bhp with the introduction of Porsche's 'Varioram' variable-length intake system. At the top of the range sat a four-wheel-drive 408bhp 911 Turbo.

With the introduction of the Boxster roadster, first seen as a concept car in 1993, Porsche had a smaller, cheaper model to slot in below the increasingly expensive 911. Boxster engineering went into the next-generation 911, the 996 series, which finally turned to water-cooled engines – ending after many years the era of air-cooled Porsches.

Porsche's range diversified still further with the introduction of the Cayenne SUV, but still Stuttgart's core business was the 911. The latest chapter in that story is the 997 series of 2004 – and with 997 cabrio and turbo models waiting in the wings, it's a story that's set to run for many years to come.

THE KING IS DEAD

In 1989 Porsche unveiled a new 911, known internally as the 964. The shape was broadly the same as before and a few components were carried over from the old car, but much was new. The suspension now used coil springs all round, the brake system incorporated ABS, and there was a new 3.6-liter, twin-ignition engine. Four-wheel drive was a feature of the first model, the Carrera 4, but a two-wheel-drive Carrera 2 followed in 1990.

SPORTS SPECIAL

'RS' is a designation that gets Porsche fans' hearts pumping. Derived from the word Rennsport, *the German term for motor racing, RS has always denoted Porsches with an extra dose of raw speed and grip, and little in the way of creature comforts. The 964-series Carrera RS (below) introduced in 1992 followed the pattern, with lightweight trim and racing-style seats, bigger wheels and tires, and a small power increase over the standard 964.*

PLUGGING THE GAP

Changing market conditions prompted Porsche to introduce a turbo version of the new 964-series 911 (right) at very short notice. So these first turbo 964s carried over the old 3.3-liter engine, now fitted with a bigger turbo and more efficient intercooler to boost power to 320bhp. In 1993 Porsche introduced a turbo version of the 3.6-liter engine boasting 360bhp, but it would be short-lived: a new 911 series was on the way.

CUP WINNERS

With interest waning in Group C racing, Porsche organized its own sports car series, first using 944 Turbos and later 964 Carrera 2s. For 1994 a new 'Cup' racer was born (previous pages), based on the latest chapter of the 911 story – the 993 series. With a 3.8-liter engine developing 315bhp, together with the 993's stiffer shell and more sophisticated rear suspension, these were the fastest Cup cars yet.

SAME BUT DIFFERENT

The 993 series (above) was still recognizably a 911, but the shape differed so much in detail that only the roof was common to the previous 964 series. The base engine was still 3.6 liters, though now developing 270bhp. At the rear of the car was a brand new multi-link suspension system, mounted on a cast aluminum subframe. The new suspension had been designed for a Porsche sports sedan, but when that project was canceled the design was adapted for the new 911.

FRESH AIR CHOICES

As before, the 996 was available in several bodystyles. In addition to the coupé there was this full Cabriolet (below), which was always popular in the sunnier states of the USA. In countries with more changeable weather a popular alternative was the latest Targa, which had an electrically operated sliding glass roof – offering much of the open-air appeal of a full cabrio, with the ability to transform itself into a snug coupé at the flick of a switch.

IT'S SHOWTIME

Porsche unveiled the prototype of a new roadster, the Boxster, in 1993. Unlike the rear-engined 911, the new car was mid-engined, with a striking new shape designed by Porsche's Dutch styling boss Harm Lagaay. Though there were hints of the 1950s 356 Speedster in the car's lines, the Boxster was a fresh and modern design – and the show car attracted admiring crowds wherever it went.

ROADSTER REVIVAL

It was inevitable that the production version of the Boxster (above) would be a little less radical than the show car, but even so it was an attractive new product for Porsche. The 2.4-liter Boxster was cheap, for a Porsche, slotting in neatly below the 911. Despite competition from such cars as the Mercedes-Benz SLK, the BMW Z3, and Audi's cult TT, the Boxster quickly won Porsche many new friends.

IMPROVING THE BREED

The turbo version of the 993 series, the 911 Turbo 4S, featured four-wheel drive, twin turbochargers, and 408bhp. For racing Porsche produced the 911 GT2 (below), with the same engine boosted to 430bhp. The GT2 was rear-wheel drive and was stripped out in the manner of previous RS models to lighten the car. Racing versions produced 480bhp as a matter of course, and later an Evolution specification for entry into the GT1 category developed over 600bhp.

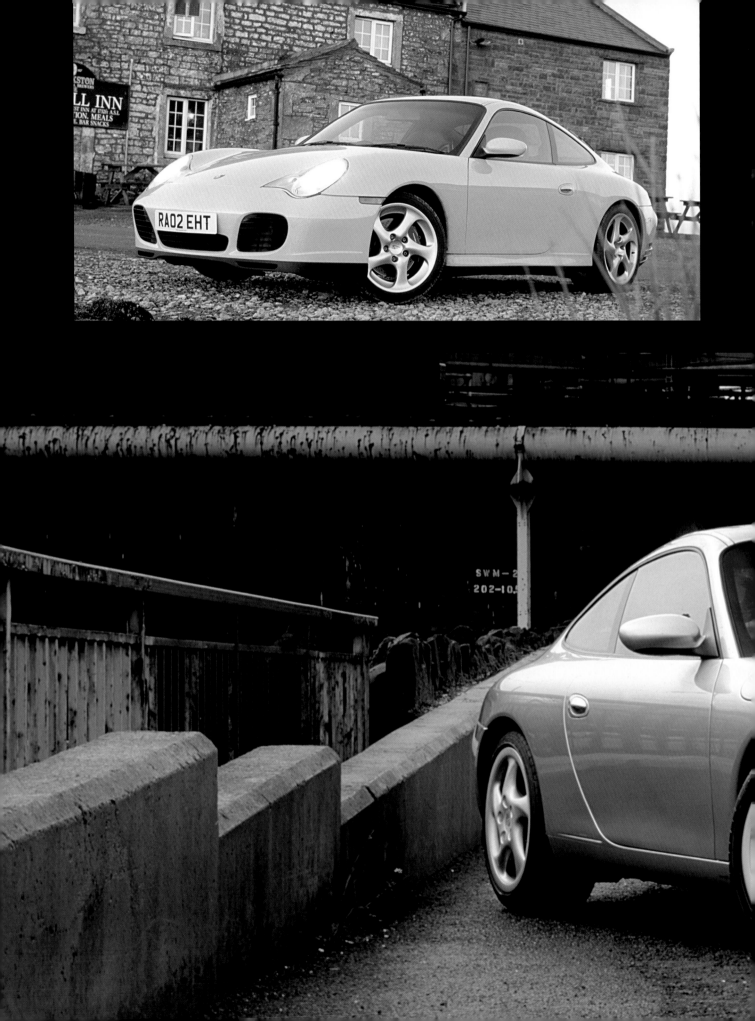

GRIP AND GRUNT

Like previous 911s, the 996 was available with two-wheel drive and four-wheel drive. The two-wheel-drive car was simply called the 911 Carrera and the normally-aspirated four-wheel-drive car was the Carrera 4 – later, after a power boost to 320bhp, the Carrera 4S (left). Four-wheel drive was also a standard feature of the latest 911 Turbo, now developing 415bhp and with a top speed only fractionally under 190mph (306km/h) – making it one of the fastest production cars in the world.

BOXTER'S BROTHER

Porsche replaced the 993 series with the 996 (below) in 1998. This new 911 was based around the Boxster's structure, just over a third of the components being common to both cars. The 996 shared the cheaper model's front-end styling, with the turn indicators and headlamp on each side integrated into a single unit. A new 3.4-liter water-cooled engine powered the 996, ending an era of air-cooled Porsches which had begun in the 1940s.

SPECIAL BREW

The 911 GT3RS of 2003 (left) was a 'homologation special,' built specifically to legalize the car for racing in a production car category. Its normally-aspirated 3.6-liter engine produced 381bhp, enough to give the lightweight GT3RS performance to match the Turbo, with a top speed of 190mph (306km/h) and 0–62mph (100km/h) acceleration in just 4.4 seconds. Like the original Carrera RS of 1973, it was available only in white, and to underline its racing pedigree a full roll cage was included in the specification.

NEW HORIZONS

Ferry Porsche once said that his company would only ever produce sports cars, but the Cayenne SUV (above) proved just how much Porsche had changed in the latter part of the 20th century. Developed in conjunction with VW (who built a cheaper version called the Touareg), the Cayenne offered the straight-line performance of a sports car, the carrying capacity of a station wagon and the go-anywhere appeal of a 4x4 truck. It was powered by a new 4.5-liter V8 engine available in both normally aspirated and turbocharged forms.

ROAD TO NOWHERE

Changes to sports car racing rules strangled Porsche's turbocharged engines, so instead it planned a new V10 motor which would derive its power from large capacity rather than turbocharging. Eventually this 5.5-liter V10 race car was canceled, but the concept lived on as the hugely expensive, super-rare Carrera GT road car (below). Production began at the Leipzig plant in 2002, with engines supplied from Zuffenhausen. Porsche planned to build just 1000 Carrera GTs.

BACK TO THE FUTURE

The latest 911, the 997 series (right), marks a return to the classic 911 shape. The fenders and air intakes are subtler than before, and the classic 'face' returns with the use of oval headlamps and separate turn indicators instead of the 996's Boxster-style units. The base 911 is now powered by a 3.6-liter, 325bhp engine giving it a top speed of 177mph (285km/h) and there's a turbo version on the way.

Jaguar's 1991 XJR-14, built for the Group C World Championship and IMSA racing in the US, later ran as a Mazda using a Judd V10 engine, and was then rebuilt with a Porsche flat-six. Porsche's works team abandoned plans to run the car, now called the WSC95, after last-minute rule changes. Eventually Porsche allowed the Joest team to run it, and Joest won Le Mans with this car in 1996 – and again in 1997.

LEADING THE PACK

After a brief flirtation with Formula 1 in the 1960s, Porsche concentrated on sports car racing. Light Zagato-bodied Carrera GTL or Abarth-Carrera coupés were raced with much success in the early 1960s, then from 1964 there was the 904 sports-racing car using the existing four-cylinder engine, the new six-cylinder from the 911, or a development of the eight-cylinder F1 engine.

The 904 sired a string of increasingly rapid sports racing cars, culminating in the 917s – which, after a shaky start, came to dominate sports car racing and delight crowds as they battled with the big V12 Ferraris. The only thing that could stop them was a change of regulations, which outlawed the 917s at the end of 1971.

Across in North America, Porsche raced in the spectacular Can-Am series. Turbocharged flat-12 engines powered the 917/10 and 917/30 cars, ultimately delivering 1100bhp and putting the Porsche name at the top of yet another form of racing.

Porsche returned to the top level of sports car racing with the 936 and the Group 5 935, and then went back into Formula 1 by producing an amazingly powerful 1.5-liter turbo engine for the McLaren team, bankrolled by Mansour Ojjeh's TAG company.

The 956/962 cars proved extraordinarily successful at Le Mans, helping to give Porsche an unmatched record in the 24-hour classic. As regulations changed so competition Porsches changed with them, and in the 1990s production supercars were the required formula – but the 962 won again in the form of the Dauer-Porsche, a pseudo-production car. Then Porsche returned with the GT1 version of the latest 911 (the 993 series) and once again made Le Mans its own.

BACK IN ACTION

Using the four-cam engine from the hottest 356s, the 904 sports car regularly trounced much bigger machinery, and it won the European 2.0-liter championship in 1964. In the Targa Florio that year two 904s streaked through the streets of Sicily ahead of Ferraris and Alfa Romeos. Antonio Pucci and Colin Davis won and this sister car of Gianni Balzarini/ Herbert Linge (above) took second place.

STIFF OPPOSITION

The long, tapering tail and bubble-like cockpit of the 907 langheck (long tail) were shaped to present the minimum air resistance, essential at Le Mans (right), with its four-mile straight but the car proved to be unstable at speed and at the last minute a tiny spoiler was added to the tail. Even so the 2.0-liter Porsches had no answer to the 4.0-liter V12 Ferrari P4s and the 7.0-liter Ford GTs: the best 907 came home fifth.

RALLY TO THE CAUSE

The versatile Vic Elford was in his element in the tricky Targa Florio, combining race-driver precision and speed out in the countryside with a rally driver's ability to cope with the slippery roads through the Sicilian villages. In 1968 Elford shared this 907 (below) with veteran Umberto Maglioli, winning by a minute despite being delayed by a puncture.

STARS AND CARS

At Sebring in 1970 this 908/02 (top) was crewed by a glamorous pair of drivers. Actor Steve McQueen (left, pictured on the right) was combining his enthusiasm for racing with 'research' for his film Le Mans. Peter Revson (pictured on the left) was the son of the founder of the Revlon cosmetics company, but despite his 'wealthy playboy' image he proved to be a capable, professional driver. The pair finished second, just 22 seconds behind the winning Ferrari.

THE PURSUIT OF POWER

More power was needed to provide Porsche with an effective rival to the Fords and Ferraris, and it came in the form of a 4.5-liter flat-12 engine, related in many ways to the earlier six- and eight-cylinder units. The slippery but unstable long-tail bodies of the early cars were later supplemented by this more manageable short-tail (or kurzheck) version, the 917K, seen here (above) in the distinctive Gulf colors of the JW Automotive team.

BRUTE FORCE

Porsche built the turbocharged 917/10 for Can-Am racing, which by 1972 was dominated by the mighty McLarens with their 8.0-liter Chevrolet V8s. Driver Mark Donahue helped develop the Penske-run car, but when Donahue was injured in a crash at Road Atlanta, George Follmer took over (above). Though it took Follmer a while to get to grips with the 917/10's tricky power delivery, he went on to win the Can-Am championship.

REVENGE OF CAPTAIN NICE

Mark Donahue's easygoing off-track persona earned him the nickname 'Captain Nice,' but there was no doubting his commitment in the cockpit. After missing part of the 1972 Can-Am series through injury, Donahue dominated the 1973 championship in the 917/30, which had better aerodynamics and better handling than previous Can-Am Porsches. By now, the turbocharged flat-12 engine developed around 1100bhp in race trim.

GROUP THERAPY

Porsche built the 934 and 935, derived from the 911 Turbo, for racing in Group 4 and Group 5 events. For 1978 a new four-valve engine was developed for a new version, the 935/78, which featured low-drag long-tail bodywork. It won its debut race, at Silverstone (below), but could finish only eighth at Le Mans. An oil leak during the race prompted the team to nurse the car slowly to the finish – ironically the leak was later found to be minor.

AIR SUPERIORITY

By 1980 Formula 1 had been taken over by 'ground effect' cars, which, in addition to upside-down wings front and rear, utilized the air flowing under the car to create downforce. The Kremer brothers applied similar techniques to the 935, producing the Le Mans-winning 935K3 (above).

THE LONGEST DAY

Belgian Jacky Ickx and Briton Derek Bell formed one of the greatest driving partnerships ever seen at Le Mans with three overall wins. On the following pages Ickx brings the 936/81 through the Ford chicane on the way to winning the 1981 race, the Belgian's fifth Le Mans victory and Porsche's sixth. The pair would repeat the triumph the following year in the new Porsche 956.

UNDER PRESSURE

Renault introduced turbocharged engines to Formula 1 in 1977, and the first turbo-powered champion was crowned in 1983. By then McLaren had decided to make the switch to turbo power, using a new V6 engine financed by Mansour Ojjeh's TAG company and designed by Porsche. Alain Prost won the turbo McLaren MP4/2's first Grand Prix victory in Brazil in March 1984 (below). Victory in the World Championship would go to team-mate Niki Lauda, just half a point ahead of Prost.

TRIUMPHS AND TRAGEDIES

Derek Bell takes over the 962 that Hans Stuck has just brought into the pits at Spa in 1985 (right). Bell would win Le Mans three times in 956/962 cars, which would become the cars to beat in Group C racing. But even Porsche's dominance of the sport in the 1980s met with trials and tragedies. That Spa race was ended early after a crash which claimed the life of Stefan Bellof, and just days later Manfred Winkelhock was killed in an accident at Mosport Park in Ontario, Canada – both driving Porsches.

PORSCHES AND PYRAMIDS

Four-wheel-drive 911s, known to the factory as 953s, entered the long-distance Paris-Dakar endurance rally in 1984, with the experienced pairing of René Metge and Dominic Lemoyne winning the event. Porsche returned in 1985, but none of the three Stuttgart entries survived to the finish. The 1986 event was more successful, Metge and Lemoyne winning in a rally-prepared 959 with this car (above) of Jacky Ickx and Claude Brasseur second.

DAUER POWER

By the early 1990s the governing body of motor sport, the FIA, was keen to introduce new rules for sports car racing favoring modified production cars rather than purpose-built 'prototypes.' But the rules left a loophole which was exploited by the Dauer-Porsche 962LM. Dauer converted 962s for road use, and it was a short step to turn one of those cars into a racing machine. Yannick Dalmas, Hurley Haywood, and Mauro Baldi won Le Mans with it in 1994 (left and below).

The works Porsche 911 GT1s had expired in the 1997 Le Mans race, leaving the door open for the Joest car – one crashed, and the other burst into flames on the Mulsanne straight. But Stuttgart made no mistake the following year: Laurent Aiello, Allan McNish, and Stéphane Ortelli won the race a lap ahead of the sister car of Jörg Müller, Uwe Alzen, and Bob Wollek.

INDEX

Abarth Carrera GTL 20, 77
Auto Union 7, 9

Behra, Jean 16
Bell, Derek 87, 90

Daimler 7, 9
Dean, James 9
Donahue, Mark 83, 84

Elford, Vic 26–27, 80–81

Follmer, George 83
Frankenburg, Richard von 13
Frère, Paul 13
Fuhrmann, Ernst 36, 38, 46

Glaser (coachbuilder) 12
Grand Prix 23, 26, 90
Gurney, Dan 23

Hoffman, Max 12

Ickx, Jacky 87, 88–89, 92

Komenda, Erwin 10,

Lagaay, Harm 67
Lauda, Niki 90
Le Mans 7, 13, 76, 77, 78, 81, 86, 87, 93, 95

McQueen, Steve 81
Monaco 22,
Monte Carlo Rally 26

Paris-Dakar Rally 57, 92
Porsche
    356 1, 8, 10, 11, 12, 19, 20, 28, 43,
    356B 16
    356B Super 90 16–17,
    356SC 18-19,
    550 Spyder 7, 9, 13, 16

718 F2 22
718 GTR 20–21
718 RSK 16, 22
901 26
904 77, 78
907 78, 79, 80
908/02 81
911 7, 24, 25–41, 43,
911 Carrera RS 1, 25, 30–31, 33, 57
911E 30
911 GT2 56, 69
911 GT3RS 72, 73
911SC 25, 36
912 28–29
914 43, 44
916 45
917 77
917/10 83
917/30 84-85
917K 82
924 36, 43, 44–45
924 Carrera GT 1
924 Turbo 47, 48
928 36, 43, 46, 53
928GT 53
928S 48
928S2 54, 55
934 86
935 36–37, 86
935/78 86
935K3 87
936 77
936/81 87, 88–89
944 36, 42, 48–49
944 Turbo 50–51
953 92
956/962 77, 90, 93
959 25, 40–41, 92
964 57, 58–59, 60–61
964 Carrera RS 60
968 43, 54, 55
968 Club Sport 55
993 2, 64, 69

996 65, 70–71
996 GTR RS 6
997 74, 75
America Roadster 12
Boxster 57, 66–67, 68
Carrera 25, 35, 71
Carrera 1600GS 8, 20
Carrera Club Sport 40, 41
Carrera GT 74–75
Cayenne SUV 57, 73
Cup racer 62–63, 64
Dauer-Porsche 77, 93
Speedster 13, 14–15, 67
Targa 38–39,
Type 64 9, 10
WSC95 76
Porsche, Ferdinand 7
Porsche, Ferry 9, 73
Prost, Alain 90

racing 3, 22, 62-63, 64, 76–95
    Can-Am 7, 35, 77, 83, 84
    Formula 1 23, 77, 87, 90
    Formula 2 22
Reutter 9, 10
Revson, Peter 81

Sauter, Heinrich 12
Scaglione, Franco 20
Scarlatti, Giorgio 16
Silverstone (racetrack) 86
Solitude (racetrack) 23
Stone, David 26–27

Targa Florio 16, 20, 33, 78, 80–81
Tiukkanen, Martti 26
Toivonen, Pauli 26

Volkswagen 7, 9, 10, 11, 43, 44, 73
von Trips, Wolfgang 22

Zagato 20
Zuffenhausen 9, 10, 33, 44, 53, 74